Mythical Creatures
FAIRIES

by Sue Gagliardi

FOCUS READERS

www.focusreaders.com

Focus Readers is distributed by North Star Editions:
sales@northstareditions.com | 888-417-0195

Produced for Focus Readers by Red Line Editorial.

Photographs ©: Atelier Sommerland/Shutterstock Images, cover, 1, 17, 25, 29; Pobytov/iStockphoto, 4–5; RomoloTavani/iStockphoto, 7; Yuri_Arcurs/iStockphoto, 8–9; NeydtStock/Shutterstock Images, 10; Liliya Kulianionak/iStockphoto, 12; JasonDoiy/iStockphoto, 14–15; Vera Petruk/Shutterstock Images, 19; PictureLake/iStockphoto, 20–21; egal/iStockphoto, 22–23; Fona/Shutterstock Images, 27

ISBN
978-1-63517-901-9 (hardcover)
978-1-64185-003-2 (paperback)
978-1-64185-205-0 (ebook pdf)
978-1-64185-104-6 (hosted ebook)

Library of Congress Control Number: 2018931702

Printed in the United States of America
Mankato, MN
May, 2018

About the Author

Sue Gagliardi writes fiction, nonfiction, and poetry for children. Her work appears in children's magazines including *Highlights Hello*, *Highlights High Five*, *Ladybug*, and *Spider*. She teaches kindergarten and lives in Hatboro, Pennsylvania, with her husband and son. She enjoys hiking in the woods and discovering fairy-like forms hidden among the trees and flowers.

TABLE OF CONTENTS

CHAPTER 1

A VISIT TO FAIRYLAND

Deep in the woods, a traveler discovers a secret land. The area is lush and green. Music fills the flower-scented air. Fairies called Little Folk fly above and around her.

A human girl wanders into fairyland.

The fairies welcome the traveler. They give her gifts of fairy food. With each delicious bite, she feels sleepier and sleepier. She is falling under the fairies' spell.

When the traveler awakes, the Little Folk are dancing around her. The fairy dance seems to last only a

FUN FACT

Fairies love music. They hold hands and dance in a circle. In stories, this is a common fairy dance.

 In some stories, fairies appear as glowing spots of light in the air.

few minutes. But with each step of the dance, years pass. The traveler can't escape. Life as she knew it will never be the same.

CHAPTER 2

FAIRY TALES

Stories of fairies appear in **folklore** around the world. In many stories, fairies are known as the Little Folk. They live in a secret world. Sometimes, humans stumble upon fairyland by accident.

Fairy tales are stories about magical creatures such as fairies.

➤ **Leprechauns are a type of fairy from Ireland.**

People have told fairy stories for thousands of years. In the **Middle Ages**, fairy stories became very popular. Stories often came from Scotland, England, and Ireland.

Most fairy **myths** take place in nature. Long ago, humans thought nature spirits lived in the woods. They told stories about these fairies to explain nature. For example, humans thought fairy dances caused flowers to grow faster. In other stories, fairies guard animals.

FUN FACT

In Irish folklore, a fairy carried stones in her apron. As she dropped the stones, mountains formed.

 Water fairies protect the animals in the water, such as frogs and fish.

They protect deer and wolves in the wild. Fairies might also guard water. They keep streams from overflowing.

Some humans thought fairies controlled the weather. In stories from Scotland, a fairy named Gentle Annie creates storms. These storms cause trouble for fishermen at sea. Another Scottish story tells of a blue-faced winter fairy. This fairy covers the land with snow.

FUN FACT

In Scottish folklore, dancing fairies formed the **northern lights**. The fairies were called Merry Dancers.

CHAPTER 3

FAIRY FORM

Fairies take many forms. In stories today, fairies tend to be small. They often have wings. But in old folklore, fairies were taller than humans. They were wingless. Many fairies were also invisible.

 Some fairies have scales and plants growing on their skin.

Oftentimes, fairies blend in with their surroundings. Woodland fairies tend to be brown and green. They blend in with leaves and trees. Water fairies are blue and green. They blend in with ponds.

Fairies are also shape-shifters. They often take the forms of animals. Some fairies appear as wolves or horses. Others look like birds. One type of fairy looks like a young girl. But she has scales and fish-like hands.

▷ **Forest fairies like to sit on the tops of mushrooms.**

According to folklore, there are many types of fairies. Undines look like humans. But they have shiny, blue-green skin. Sylph fairies are invisible. They glow as they fly. Other fairies are not so beautiful.

Barquests have horns, claws, and big teeth.

The brownie is a Scottish fairy that lives in humans' houses. These fairies stand 3 feet (0.9 m) tall. Brownies have shaggy hair. And they often dress in raggedy brown clothes.

FUN FACT

The Gooseberry Wife is a fairy that appears as a giant, hairy caterpillar. She guards gooseberry patches.

A brownie washes dishes in a human's home.

Fairies' appearances help them hide from humans. Since fairies can take any form, they are hard to spot. In stories, humans often do not recognize fairies.

FAIRIES TODAY

Real-life fairies exist in the form of insects. Fairyflies are tiny, winged insects. *Tinkerbella nana* is a type of fairyfly. It was named after characters in *Peter Pan*. In this story, Tinker Bell is a fairy. And Nana is a dog.

Tinkerbella nana lives in Costa Rica. The insect is less than 0.01 inches (0.03 cm) long. This is not much wider than a human hair. The fairyfly is barely visible to the human eye. *Tinkerbella nana* is a **parasite**. However, farmers like the insect. It eats pests that ruin the farmers' crops.

Tinker Bell is Peter Pan's best fairy friend.

CHAPTER 4

LIFE AS A FAIRY

Fairies live in secret. They only reveal themselves to humans when they want to. However, many fairies like the company of other fairies. Trooping fairies live in groups. Solitary fairies live alone.

 Fairies often live together in large, hollowed-out trees.

Fairies are skilled in many **trades**. Common fairy jobs include **spinning**, weaving, and cooking. Fairies often sing while they work. And they always clean up. They like things to be neat and orderly.

Fairies depend on humans for many things. For example, fairies

FUN FACT

Knockers are fairies that work in mines. They knock on the walls to lead humans toward silver and gold.

 Many fairies enjoy playing instruments such as the flute.

may borrow grain to make cakes.

They also borrow tools for their

trades. They might take spinning

wheels and weaving looms.

Some fairies are kind and generous. But others like to cause trouble. To trick humans, fairies use a magic power called glamour. Glamour makes humans see things that are not real. Breaking the spell can be hard. It requires an **ointment** made of four-leaf clovers. Humans rub the ointment on their eyes.

FUN FACT

In old folklore, fairies flew on broomsticks like witches.

 In some stories, humans become friends with fairies.

In fairy stories, humans must be careful. They don't know if they can trust fairies. They might fall under fairy spells. Or they might get lost in fairyland forever.

FOCUS ON
FAIRIES

Write your answers on a separate piece of paper.

1. Write a sentence that describes the main idea of Chapter 3.

2. Why do you think fairy stories are so popular? Which fairy story is your favorite?

3. Which type of fairy is invisible?
   - **A.** sylph
   - **B.** barquest
   - **C.** trooper

4. In fairy stories, how do humans get stuck in fairyland?
   - **A.** They choose to stay.
   - **B.** They turn into fairies.
   - **C.** They fall under a fairy spell.

5. What does **controlled** mean in this book?

*Some humans thought fairies **controlled** the weather. In stories from Scotland, a fairy named Gentle Annie created storms.*

    A. feared

    B. followed

    C. had power over

6. What does **shape-shifters** mean in this book?

*Fairies are also **shape-shifters**. They often take the forms of animals.*

    A. creatures that can change their own form

    B. creatures that turn humans into animals

    C. creatures that turn animals into humans

Answer key on page 32.

GLOSSARY

folklore
Fictional stories that people pass down over the years.

Middle Ages
A period in European history that lasted from the 400s CE to the 1400s CE.

myths
Well-known, fictional stories common to a group of people.

northern lights
A natural display of colorful lights in the night sky.

ointment
A skin cream used for medical purposes.

parasite
An animal or plant that lives on or in another living thing.

spinning
Using a spinning wheel to turn fibers into thread or yarn.

trades
Jobs that require special skills or training.

TO LEARN MORE

BOOKS

Breslin, Theresa. *An Illustrated Treasury of Scottish Mythical Creatures*. Edinburgh: Floris Books, 2015.

Maloney, Alison. *Fairies: A Spotter's Handbook*. London: Carlton Kids, 2016.

Sautter, A. J. *A Field Guide to Elves, Dwarves, and Other Magical Folk*. Mankato, MN: Capstone Press, 2015.

NOTE TO EDUCATORS

Visit **www.focusreaders.com** to find lesson plans, activities, links, and other resources related to this title.

INDEX